OPENED

GREAT SUBJECT LINES FOR
HIGHER EMAIL OPEN RATES

NATHAN LITTLETON

© Nathan Littleton 2017

ISBN 978-1-326-99478-5

All rights reserved. No part of this publication may be reproduced, distributed, or transmitted in any form or by any means, including photocopying, recording, or other electronic or mechanical methods, without the prior written permission of the publisher.

Whilst the publisher has taken all reasonable care in the preparation of this book, the publisher makes no representation, express or implied, with regard to the accuracy of the information contained in this book and cannot accept any legal responsibility or liability for any errors or omissions from the book or the consequences thereof.

Products or services that are referred to in this book may be either trademarks and/or registered trademarks of their respective owners. The publisher and author make no claims to these trademarks.

Every effort has been made to contact companies whose text I've quoted to gain their permission to include them in this publication.

A CIP catalogue record for this book is available from the British Library.

The moral rights of the author have been asserted.

CONTENTS

INTRODUCTION																5

WHAT MAKES A GOOD SUBJECT LINE?												9

AVOIDING THE DREADED SPAM FILTERS												19

MEASURING SUCCESS																21

171 SUBJECT LINES YOU CAN USE												33

EXTRA INGREDIENTS																45

COMMON MISTAKES																49

BONUS: CALL TO ACTION TEXT												55

ABOUT THE AUTHOR																59

INTRODUCTION

Whilst other marketing methods come and go, email marketing has remained a constant for decades, and it's showing no signs of going away. Put simply, email marketing is the single most effective way of reaching a large number of people in a short space of time. Nothing else compares to it, and that's what makes it so successful for so many businesses who are using it in the right way.

However, we're communicating with prospects who are much savvier than they've ever been before. They're more likely to distinguish a mass email from a personal one; they're more likely to disengage from what you're saying if it doesn't interest them; and they're far more likely to delete your carefully-crafted emails than open and read them. With all this in mind, you could be forgiven for thinking that email marketing isn't as effective as it once was, but that couldn't be further from the truth. To get positive results, we simply have to work smarter. It is often quite small tweaks that can make the difference between whether an email campaign is effective or not. But by making those small tweaks, we can reap the rewards of a unique marketing machine: one where each and every time you send an email, you know that it will generate enquiries or sales for your business. Even for those that don't buy, you stay at the forefront of their mind for when they need what you have to offer.

Maybe I'm preaching to the converted. If you're reading a book about how to write effective subject lines, I'm guessing you're already convinced about how effective email marketing can be, and you're looking to get the very best results by maximising your open rates.

The subject line is a very small tweak, but it's one that has a huge impact on the results you get from your email campaigns. A common mistake made by many people is to underestimate just how important an email's subject line is. Even many experienced marketers will craft their email content; double check that the links all go where they're supposed to; assess the best time to send their campaign; and then undo all of their hard work by using a poor subject line such as 'Special offer' or 'September Newsletter' without giving it a second thought.

Sixty-four per cent of people say that they open an email because of the subject line, and along with the 'From' name, it's the most influential factor in determining your open rates, so it's something that's definitely worth paying attention to. There's little point in crafting a wonderfully written email if it will never get opened and read, and the only way to get your email opened and read is to create a compelling subject line which invites the reader in. Of course, there are other factors that influence the open rates of your emails; if your subscriber list is old or un-nurtured (cold), your open rates will probably be poor, even with the greatest will - or subject line - in the world.

I'm fascinated by the psychological factors of which subject lines work and which ones don't. Throughout the years I've been creating email campaigns, some subject lines have worked remarkably well, and some have been absolute stinkers, too! When I sat down to work out the reasons why some worked better than others, I had to put myself in the shoes of my readers. Here's what I realised:

- They're busy, and I can be pretty certain that reading my email wasn't at the top of their to-do list.
- Their inbox is more than likely filled with other emails, many that they'll see as much more important than the one I've sent them, and a few that may even be similar or from my competitors.
- People respond better to messages that appear to be just for them. They don't want to be misled.
- As well as being busy, with their mind on other things, they probably have limited time. Perhaps they're checking their emails between meetings or while waiting for something, perhaps even while sitting on the toilet (a survey reported that three quarters of people have emailed, texted, played with apps or used the Internet - all while sitting on the

www.nathanlittleton.co.uk

loo). On average, a person takes three seconds to decide whether they should open an email, so that doesn't give us much time to make a good impression.

Knowing these things helped me to create a few rules around what makes a good subject line, and I'll share those with you to help you to write better subject lines that lead to far better results.

Some of the best inspiration for subject lines can come from your own email inbox. See what subject lines have been used in messages you've received and ask yourself specifically what it was that made you open one email, or not open another.

WHAT MAKES A GOOD SUBJECT LINE?

Let's step back for a second. To know whether a subject line is good or not, we need a barometer of success. At a basic level, I know my subject line has been successful if I get a great open rate (a statistic that modern email marketing apps include in their reports), but there's little point in comparing my rates to those of another business, whether they're in the same industry or not, as the circumstances, size and quality of the list will all be different. A fairer idea of a great open rate is whether you've made an improvement on your last campaign. If the open rate increases with every campaign you send, you know you're writing good subject lines.

A successful subject line leads to more opens, but can also lead to a higher 'read' rate - a statistic that can't be accurately measured - i.e. the number of people who open, and then read the content of, your email, as a percentage of the number of people who you send to. Naturally, you need your email to be read to invoke the action you want the reader to take. Don't automatically assume that anyone who opens your email has read it, for a few reasons:

www.nathanlittleton.co.uk

- The reported number of opens isn't strictly accurate: some of those will represent people who have simply clicked on your email to stop it from appearing as unread in their inbox.
- When a user opens an email with the intention of finding out what's inside, they'll either skim read it or read it properly. A successful subject line increases the number of people who fully read your email rather than skim read it. But you can't know which they've done from that plain statistic.

Different people will respond well to different subject lines, but there are some generalised principles we can follow to craft a great subject line:

Be interesting
This goes without saying, surely? Well you may be surprised just how many bland, boring, vanilla subject lines are being used in email campaigns every single day. Your subject line should contain something that will catch your readers' attention, by containing one or more of these elements:

- something they wouldn't expect to see
- something that will benefit them
- something that will catch them off guard

Example: *What Jennifer Aniston taught me about car leasing*

Be intriguing

Remember, your purpose in crafting a subject line is to do enough that the recipient wants to open and read your email. The rest of your aims can be taken care of within the email's content.

Time and time again, I see email campaigns where the writer has given too much away by including the highlights of their entire message in the subject line. I can understand why they'd think that's the right thing to do - traditionally the subject line is used to explain the essence of what you have to say - but it just isn't smart marketing.

Some of the best subject lines I've used have been those that have told the recipient very little about what's to follow, but have been intriguing enough to encourage them to want to find out more. However, there's a fine line between intriguing your reader and misleading them. An intriguing subject line has a positive effect when it's relevant to the content inside the email, especially when you make reference to the subject line in the message's first line.

Example:

Subject line: *I'm in a spot of bother*

First line of message: *I've got a real problem here. There are three cars on our forecourt which are about to go to auction, and as I know you're in the market for a new saloon car, I wanted to make*

*sure you didn't miss out before someone at the auction house
snapped up your perfect car.*

A subject line such as this will work especially well if you've
collected information about a prospect's buying interests and
stored them as a custom field. In this case, it's the type of car that
they're searching for. A campaign can then be sent to a segment
of the list where the custom field which represents the type of
car the prospect is interested in matches 'saloon'.

Be personal
Some subject lines I've seen great results from are those that
make an email appear as though it's been written just for each
individual recipient. For the most part, this is achieved by using
an informal, conversational style of language which mimics the
day-to-day emails that you send to your contacts.

*"Personalised emails generated 42.7% more click-throughs
on average to the web copy than non-personalised emails.
Personalised emails generated 403% more sales on average than
non-personalised emails. Personalised emails generated 42.8%
fewer unsubscribes on average than non-personalised emails."* - Jay
Conrad Levinson, Guerrilla Marketing

Knowing that a good subject line must be interesting, intriguing
and personal, we're fortunate that modern email marketing
systems provide a tool that can make your subject lines that little

bit better: including the recipient's name. It's a tool which should be used carefully, but which can dramatically increase your open rates. All modern email marketing systems allow you to include the recipient's name with a merge tag, but the exact code that you need will vary from system to system.

For example, in Campaign Monitor, there's a button marked 'Insert personalisation' in the subject line field, from which you can choose 'Insert first name'. It'll add this code to your subject line:

OPENED

[firstname,fallback=customer]

The 'fallback=customer' portion of this code represents what will be included in the subject line if there's no name stored for a subscriber. It's important to replace the 'customer' part with something that will sound natural, or with nothing at all, as in the first example below.

Example with merge tag: *Thanks [firstname,fallback=]*
Example with name included: *Thanks James*
Example if no name is stored with a record: *Thanks*

Example with merge tag: *I thought you should know [firstname,fallback=about this]*
Example with name included: *I thought you should know James*
Example if no name is stored with a record: *I thought you should know about this*

The merge tag code you need to use may be different in your email marketing application of choice, so remember to check the documentation first, and then test it afterwards to make sure it works as expected.

Be genuine
We want our subject lines to be interesting and intriguing, but it's important to set the right expectations. You can't promise free fluffy kittens for everybody in your subject line just to generate

an open, attractive though it is, if you're not going to deliver on it. We don't want to mislead readers, and we definitely do want to keep them on our side. It's still possible to use email marketing effectively without resorting to dark tactics. Or fluffy kittens.

Be succinct
"Subject lines with fewer than 50 characters get 12.5% higher open rates" – Constant Contact

Subject lines need to be short for two main reasons:

- More than half of all emails are now opened on mobile devices, and that's only increasing. What's interesting about emails received on mobile devices is that the subject line is often truncated to around 30-35 characters, so there's no point in creating a wonderful but long subject line if only the first portion is ever going to get seen.
- People are busy! They don't want to read lots of text. They want to know what you have to say so they can decide whether they should open your email or hit the delete button. Clear and concise is the only way to go.

One of the simplest and yet most effective subject lines I've seen came from Barack Obama's campaign for re-election, and simply read "Hey". Of course, the 'Barack Obama' sender name will have played a large part in this subject line's success, but you have to marvel at the simplicity of it.

Use the right voice for your business

As a conference speaker, I share my email marketing methodology from the stage in keynote sessions, workshops and masterclasses. Some of my favourite sessions to run are live demonstrations, where over the course of an hour or two, I create a campaign from the stage, taking in the thoughts and contributions of the audience and creating an email that is then sent to a list belonging to a willing audience member, arranged in advance.

During one of these sessions for a shipping firm, I'd written a campaign which was going to be sent to the list of a willing audience member who had agreed to be my guinea-pig for the day. This campaign had a few key goals:

- warm up the list that hadn't been emailed to in a couple of years
- remind subscribers of who the sender was
- let subscribers know that they'd be receiving expert tips and advice over the weeks that followed
- ask if they had a package they needed delivering right away

We arrived at the point of choosing the subject line, and I asked people to volunteer what they thought would make a good subject line (based on being interesting, intriguing, personal, genuine and succinct). There were some good suggestions but the one I thought was best caused a little controversy. The subject line in question was:

'How big's your package?'

It was met with a mixture of both laughs and shaking heads from the 100 or so people in the room. Many people thought it was a subject line that would catch people's attention, whilst others considered it unprofessional.

Personally, I loved it, and I'm certain that in this context it would lead to a very high open rate. That said, I can definitely see why some people didn't like it, and I can also see why some people might decide not to use it in their own campaigns. Whether you're a single-person business or a multi-national conglomerate, your business is a brand which has an identity, a personality and voice. Every piece of marketing you write is a representation of that voice, so it has to reflect the perception you want people to have of your organisation.

For some businesses, a subject line such as that is perfectly fitting with the voice and personality their brand portrays, while for others, it may be a step too far. Sometimes we have to do the things that are necessary to stand out from the crowd, and some of those things can be controversial, but how far you're prepared to go is up to you.

AVOIDING THE DREADED SPAM FILTERS

Our spam filters stop us from receiving requests from people who are desperate to put millions of dollars into our bank accounts. They also stop us knowing how we can satisfy our lovers in every way imaginable. Unfortunately, they can also prevent emails that we want to receive from ever reaching our inboxes. They work by scanning a message for elements that they consider to be similar to those found in unsolicited messages from spammers.

This means that certain words earn emails a higher spam score, and the higher the spam score, the more likely your email is to never reach the inbox at all, but rather be destined for the junk mailbox. Words and phrases such as "viagra", "extra income", "weight loss" and "increased girth" are the obvious culprits, and unless you're in genuine industries related to those terms, it's unlikely that you'd feel compelled to use them.

However, there are a few spam trigger words and phrases that may surprise you, such as 'free', 'click here', 'sale', 'call' and 'deal'. It's important to bear this in mind when you're choosing the words for your email's subject line. Whilst using them won't automatically send your email into your recipients' spam box (in fact, some of them are included in the examples in this book), the more of them you use, the higher the chance that that will happen.

THERE ARE A FEW SPAM TRIGGER WORDS AND PHRASES THAT MAY SURPRISE YOU, SUCH AS 'FREE', 'CLICK HERE', 'SALE', 'CALL' AND 'DEAL'.

MEASURING SUCCESS

There are only a small number of marketing methods that can give you an in-depth analysis of how a campaign is performing with up-to-the-minute data. When you use a dedicated provider such as Campaign Monitor, MailChimp or Constant Contact, email marketing is one of those few. Within their reporting suites, you'll find a number of useful statistics.

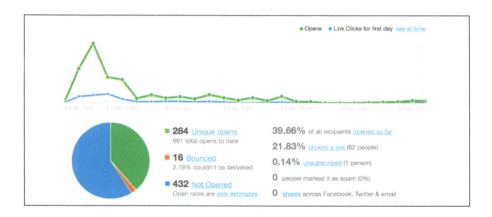

Here are some of the main ones explained:

Opens and unique opens

Your open rate is the percentage of the emails that have been delivered that are opened by your recipients. It's a useful metric for understanding your list's quality when you've sent your first campaign, and also how effective your subject lines are compared to previous campaigns.

It's worth noting that in order to record 'opens', a small, invisible tracking image is embedded within your email. When the application used to display the email (Outlook, Apple Mail, Gmail) requests the tracking image, the recipient is marked as having opened the email. However, many email applications block images from being displayed for security reasons, with the user then prompted to enable images should they choose to do so. For an open to be recorded, they'd then need to either enable the images, or interact with the email by clicking on a link. For that reason, open rates are intended as a guide, rather than an absolute statistic, but they continue to be useful in allowing you to compare your open rates from one campaign to the next.

A unique open is exactly as the name would suggest. As an email can be opened more than once (and it is possible to see how many times a recipient opened your email), a unique open is an indication of how many people opened your email. For example, if John Smith opens your email twice, Mary Baker opens your email six times, and Louise Berry opens your email once, that's nine opens. The number of unique opens is three.

Open rates cannot be tracked or measured when you're sending plain text campaigns (emails with no images , links or or fancy formatting). Because it's impossible to include a tracking image in a plain text email, there's no way of being able to record whether an email was opened.

Here are the main factors which will influence the number of opens that you get:

- Your 'From' name and email address, and whether people recognise it.
- Your subject line
- The quality of your list (in terms of valid addresses and relevance to your market)
- The size of your list
- Your email's spam score
- The time of day and day of the week you send your email

Clicks and unique clicks
A click is recorded when a recipient clicks on a link to a web page within your email. You're able to see how many people clicked on links, exactly who clicked on those links and which links they clicked on.

Clicks are measured by replacing your actual link with a tracking link. When a user clicks on a link in your email, they're taken to a special, hidden page provided by your email marketing

OPENED

provider. Their click is recorded, and then they're taken off to where you intended.

Unique clicks are slightly more complicated than unique opens.

- John Smith clicks link 1 once and link 2 three times
- Mary Baker clicks link 1 twice but doesn't click link 2
- Louise Berry clicks link 1 five times and link 2 twice

The example above represents an email with two links. It's had thirteen clicks and five unique clicks because two people clicked on both links, and one person only clicked on the one.

Here are the main factors which will influence the number of clicks that you get:

- The quality of your list (in terms of valid addresses and relevance to your market)
- The size of your list
- How many people opened your email in the first place
- How many people actually read your email
- Whether recipients know, like and trust you
- How interesting and persuasive your message is
- How interesting and persuasive the link itself is
- Whether people care about what the link is (relevance to your market again)

Bounces

Bounces are email addresses that couldn't be delivered to. This can happen for a number of reasons, and if you're working with a list that you haven't communicated with for a while, you may find that the number of bounces you get is quite high.

You can reduce the number of bounces in your campaigns by sending emails regularly and by using data that you know for sure is clean (checking for typos before you import your data can help).

You can access a list of bounces for your campaign within the reports in your email marketing app.

There are two main kinds of bounce:

Soft bounce

A soft bounce happens when your message is received by the recipient's email server (because the email address is valid), but it's rejected before it's received by your recipient. This might happen because their inbox is full, the server is having problems, the message is too large or it's been blocked as spam.

Email marketing providers deal with this kind of bounce in a clever way: they'll keep the person on your list and they'll be included in a small number of future campaigns (usually between 2 and 5): if they continue to bounce, they'll be removed from

www.nathanlittleton.co.uk

your list, which means that the number of bounces you get will decrease over time, and you're not paying to send emails to people who will never receive them.

Hard bounce
A hard bounce is an email that has been rejected by your recipient's email server because it is permanently undeliverable. The main reasons for this are invalid addresses or addresses that no longer exist.

Hard bounces are unfixable without manually confirming that the addresses are valid, and these email addresses will be automatically removed from your lists by your email marketing provider, so they won't receive any future campaigns that you send.

Unsubscribes
Every time you send a mass email using a dedicated email marketing provider, an unsubscribe link is included so that anyone who doesn't wish to hear from you again can remove themselves from your mailing list. Naturally, we want to keep this number as low as possible, but unsubscribes aren't necessarily a bad thing:

- With every unsubscribe, the quality of your list improves, meaning that a higher percentage of the people who remain on your list do want to hear from you as they begin to know, like and trust you. In addition, you're then only paying to send to the people who want to hear from you.

- Some people will unsubscribe if you have more than one email address on record for them. No matter how good your emails are, people only need to receive them once for them to be effective!
- Not everyone will like you. And that's OK. Every email address has a real person behind it, and although that person was once interested in your business, they may have lost interest or found something that they feel is better than what you have to offer. More often than not, they wouldn't have purchased from you anyway.
- The more you can learn about which content leads to a high unsubscribe rate, the more you can improve your future campaigns.

You can access a list of people who have unsubscribed from your list within the reports in your email marketing app.

Spam reports
This metric indicates how many people marked your email as being spam, which means that they either didn't give you permission to email them in the first place, they don't remember giving you permission, or they don't really know what spam is so they'll hit the button anyway because your email annoyed them. It's important that this number is as low as possible, because a high number of spam complaints can lead to your account being closed.

OPENED

Campaign Monitor offers the following tips for reducing the chances of your campaigns being reported as spam:

- *Use our confirmed opt-in subscribe process to ensure a high-quality subscriber list. This also provides proof that those making spam complaints are unwarranted.*
- *Add a clear explanation at the top of every email you send that explains how you got that subscriber's permission, and give them the opportunity to unsubscribe immediately if they no longer wish to hear from you.*
- *Don't wait for too long after people subscribe to send your first email, because recipients may forget opting in by the time they hear from you and report the email as spam.*
- *Set clear expectations when someone joins your list. Tell them what you'll be sending them and how often.*

The importance of keeping the number of spam reports to an absolute minimum is another reason why it isn't advisable to buy data lists or scrape email addresses from websites. While this kind of data is usually legal (when purchased from a legitimate source), because they may have opted in to receive communications from third parties, they haven't specifically asked to hear from you, so the likelihood of receiving a spam complaint is increased because they don't recognise who you are.

Measuring successful subject lines
I might be stating something obvious here, but you want

28   www.nathanlittleton.co.uk

your open and click rates to be as high as possible, and your unsubscribe and spam report rates to be as low possible. The subject line you choose for a campaign is going to have the biggest effect on your open rate, but it can also affect your click rate (if your subject line interests them enough to read and take action on your email rather than just open and skim read it) and your unsubscribe/spam report rate (if they feel misled by your subject line or the content wasn't as interesting as the subject line led them to believe it would be!).

Not all open rates are equal
One of the most common questions I'm asked is "what's a good open rate?" My answer is always the same: a good open rate is one which is higher than the one you got on your last campaign. If you get a higher open rate than you got on your last campaign, that means the quality of your list is improving and you've chosen a good subject line.

I'm sure that doesn't feel like a particularly helpful answer. What they really want to hear is "the average is 20%" or "most people get between 30% and 40%," and they can feel suitably smug or downbeat depending on how their own open rates compare. The problem with those kinds of answers is they won't serve you. Everyone has different size lists, in various different niches, built up over different amounts of time, with different relationships to the senders, who in turn have different personalities and different products and services to sell. With

www.nathanlittleton.co.uk

that in mind, it doesn't make sense to compare your open rates to anyone else's.

If you haven't sent an email campaign before, send one. Then you'll have an open rate to compare to. If you're using email marketing already, test and measure the small tweaks you make on each campaign to get a better result every time.

Squeezing out the extra juice
I'm a big believer in testing and measuring the results of my marketing to make sure I'm getting the best results I can, and you should be too! Subject lines are no different, and modern email marketing systems have a facility that makes this really easy, which is known as either a 'split test', or an 'A/B split test'. If you're in two minds about which subject line to use, or if you just want to get the best possible result, you can run a test with two subject lines to a small portion of your list (you can set the size of that portion yourself).

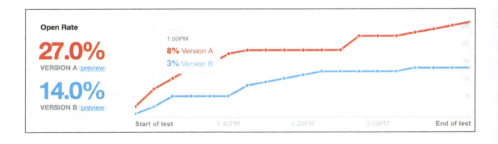

For example, on a list containing 1,000 subscribers, we might set the test size to 10%, which means that each subject line will be sent to 5% of the list. Subject line A will be sent to 50 people and subject line B will be sent to 50 people. The winning subject line will then be used for the campaign, and sent to the remainder of the list automatically, based on which one generated the best result. You can choose how the winner is determined, either by which one resulted in the best open rate, or by which one led to the most clicks through to a particular link.

This is a really useful tool, and one which I would suggest using as often as you can until you're comfortable with crafting really great subject lines.

THE WINNING SUBJECT LINE WILL THEN BE USED FOR THE CAMPAIGN, AND SENT TO THE REMAINDER OF THE LIST AUTOMATICALLY, BASED ON WHICH ONE GENERATED THE BEST RESULT."

171 SUBJECT LINES YOU CAN USE

've curated this list to inspire you to create better subject lines for your own emails. Feel free to tweak, adapt or even simply copy them to use in your own campaigns.

In many of the examples, I've included words that are relevant to lots of different kinds of businesses and industries so you can see how they apply to anyone. Adjust them to fit your own needs.

Benefits
A subject line that simply explains the benefits of what you have to say plucks the very essence from the psychology of marketing. You're explaining how your reader can gain, save or accomplish something. Knowing your target market and understanding what challenges or opportunities they have makes it much easier to create benefits-based subject lines that work.

Examples
- Kate - I've got a free VIP ticket for you
- Here you go - on the house
- Something for you
- You've been upgraded

www.nathanlittleton.co.uk

- A gift for you
- Your invitation
- A special invitation
- No cost, no catch
- Done for you
- Please find attached

How-tos

A 'how-to' subject line should be used on emails where you're providing a solution to a challenge or opportunity that your reader has, in the form of an educational article, a quick tip or even a product or service you're offering. It should include a reference to the specific challenge or opportunity you're helping with, and if the reader identifies with it, they'll want to read more.

Knowing your market and having a high-quality list that's filled with the right kind of people will make this type of subject line even more successful.

Examples

- How to create subject lines that get higher open rates
- How to double your Twitter following in just 7 days
- How to relieve your back pain today
- How to create an extra 3 hours per week in just 17 minutes
- How to sell your car stress-free

- How to overcome your networking nerves
- If we had to build a business in just 3 days, here's what we'd do
- If you need a cash flow boost, here's what to do
- What to do when HMRC visits
- What to do with friends this weekend

Negative outcome avoidance

It's often easier to motivate someone away from something negative than it is to motivate them towards a positive scenario, and that's why these subject lines work well. You're painting a picture of a fear or bad situation your recipients could face in the near future and, as an added bonus, hinting that what follows in your email will give them the solution to avoid it.

Examples

- Don't make the same mistake I did
- Most common mistakes people make at Christmas
- What to do when disaster strikes on 5th June
- 6 stage faux-pas and how to avoid them
- CRINGE! Embarrassing for him, but not for you
- They always make this mistake
- You've probably got more patience than me
- You're not alone
- It took me 15 tries! Here's how I cracked it.
- I think there's a problem

Scarcity and urgency

Great for sales emails, this type of subject line takes advantage of your readers' fear of missing out. By using words and phrases that suggest time is of the essence, you give your readers a reason to open your email, read your content and take action now rather than waiting until a later date or until they receive another email from you.

Examples

- Last chance
- Don't miss out
- Don't miss this
- Ends in 2 hours and 3 minutes
- Only 24 hours left
- Just 4 remaining
- Bad news
- Reminder
- Almost gone
- You're missing out
- Expires at midnight
- Last one
- All gone...
- Sold out! But...
- They're going quicker than I thought

Commands

Commands in subject lines are useful for getting actions quickly, and they're most effective when you know how they fit within a sequence of emails. They tend to imply that the next step for something to happen is a quick and easy one, so your recipients are more likely to do what you say more quickly.

Examples

- Choose a colour
- Read this first
- Please read this now
- What to do next
- First step
- Next step
- Complete your application
- Just tick this box
- It's your turn now
- I need one thing from you
- You missed this step
- Response required
- Awaiting response

Teasers

Teaser subject lines can be some of the most effective, and are used simply to generate curiosity. They should be interesting and intriguing enough that the reader wants to find out what you're

OPENED

about to say. Don't give too much away, just enough that you pique their interest.

Examples
- You've got great taste
- Sneak preview
- Sneak peek
- I hope I'm not too late with this
- Well this is embarrassing
- Don't open this email
- Coming soon
- Look what I've got planned
- Coming up
- Thinking of you
- I'm panicking
- Hey
- Red or green?
- I saw this and thought of you
- I shouldn't tell you this
- Just a quick one
- Hmm...
- We're throwing a party!
- A bare-faced bribe
- I'll be there
- Announcement
- A special announcement
- Great news

- My personal favourite
- Cancelled!
- I've been caught with my pants down
- You're going to love this
- Probably won't work
- My mistake
- Yes!
- You should see this
- My bad
- Personal
- Private
- Confidential
- Guess where I am
- OMG
- WTF
- LOL
- Meeting
- Let's meet
- Dates
- Feedback
- Quick question
- Oops
- To do
- Thanks
- Thank you
- I'm so grateful
- I can explain

Mimicking

As an experienced email marketer, I can't help but smile when I see a subject line that catches *me* off guard. This happened when I received an email from an online meat delivery company called Muscle Food. The subject line they used was 'Muscle Food shared "95p_Steak_Mince.mp4" with you'. It caught me off guard because it follows the same structure that Dropbox and other file sharing sites use when they notify you that someone has sent you something.

It got me thinking that there are a number of other possible subject lines that could be used that follow a similar train of thought.

However, I must offer a word of warning: the aim is certainly not to make your recipients think you are someone else, completely pass yourself off as another company or website, or trick them. The aim is simply to catch their attention.

Examples

- Nathan Littleton shared "Marketing-Workshop.mp4" with you
- (no subject)
- Sales tips eBook - invitation to view
- Your book has been shipped
- Thanks for your purchase
- Your review: Deluxe Wine and Roses Gift Hamper

Lists

Lists are great for structuring articles and packaging up valuable content in a way that's easy to digest. People know that, and while it's important to be careful that you don't give too much away too soon with this type of subject line, they're very effective because they demonstrate value.

Examples

- 5 reasons why your LinkedIn profile is dull
- 12 big mistakes businesses make when choosing a virtual assistant
- Forty-five ways to create passive revenue
- Revealed: My 5 secrets to working less and being paid more
- 14 people who wish they'd planned ahead
- 6 ways to save on your utility bills
- Five steps to building muscle mass
- The 8 main reasons why you're losing sales online
- 16 home video production tips from the pros

Mismatches and odd sentences

These subject lines are intriguing because they contain two things that are unrelated to each other or are just plain weird. Of course, they have to be relevant to the content of your email, so it makes sense to have an anecdote or example to write about before you create one of these subject lines.

Examples

- Delia Smith taught me how to sell!
- Penguins and the Prime Minister
- What I learnt about marketing from the strawberry man
- What Jennifer Aniston taught me about car leasing
- Boris Johnson inspired my sales process
- The Queen's guide to web development
- Why Ann Widdecombe is an amazing dancer
- What you can learn by studying sheep shearers
- My golf swing romance
- I took my dog on a date

Questions

Questions make great subject lines, especially when used in conjunction with other subject line types. Psychologically, a question opens a loop that your readers may want to close, either by answering it or finding out why you have asked it.

Examples

- Have you ever... ?
- What changed?
- What are you doing on 16th June?
- Did you see this?
- Is this for you?
- What next?
- Can I ask you something?

- What's up?
- Where are you?
- Can you do me a favour?
- Are you bored?
- Lunch?
- Coffee?
- Have you got a minute?
- Can you spare me 5 mins?
- Is everything OK?
- Really?
- Did you read it?
- Have you given up on finding a gym?
- Have you heard?
- Can you use this?
- Have you made a decision?
- Can I get your opinion?
- What happened?
- Do you need any help?

Targeted

With targeted subject lines, your aim is to build intrigue by addressing a specific audience by industry, location or group. If your readers identify with the target you've used, they're more likely to open your email.

OPENED

If you want these to be really effective, use them in combination with targeted lists and collect specific data about your customers and prospects using custom fields in your email marketing app.

Examples
- Just for London solicitors
- Attention florists
- Hey, are you an accountant?
- Made for plumbers
- 5* sales process for speakers and trainers
- Success secrets for mumpreneurs
- Properties wanted in the NG17 area
- Why dads love us
- The Audi A4 Sport 2.0 you were looking at
- I'm looking for a web designer
- Best babysitters in Devon
- Did you find an electrician?
- For your perfect wedding

EXTRA INGREDIENTS

t's a good idea to mix and match some of the subject line types here to create really powerful ones. As you create your own, here are a few other elements you might want to include to improve your subject lines even further.

[PDF] [BOOK] [VIDEO] [AUDIO] [FORM]
I've seen great results from adding a little prefix to subject lines that explains the media type that you're sharing. This is especially useful with media types that are perceived to have a higher value than others (such as BOOK and AUDIO).

Example: *[VIDEO] I took my dog on a date*

Tell me you wouldn't open an email with that subject line...

Personalisation
You can increase the impact of many of the subject lines in this book by including the recipient's name or other piece of information about them (use your email marketing provider's custom fields and merge tags to do this). If your email marketing app gives you the option to specify a fallback in case there is no name stored on a subscriber's record,

you should specify something that will sound as natural as possible.

Example with merge tag: *Did you see this [firstname,fallback=earlier]?*
Example with name included: *Did you see this Steve?*
Example if no name is stored with a record: *Did you see this earlier?*

The merge tag code you need to use may be different in your email marketing app of choice, so remember to check the documentation first, and then test it afterwards to make sure it works as expected.

Exact numbers

Specificity makes what you're saying more credible, and using unusual numbers rather than rounded figures builds curiosity.

Example: *This mistake cost me £8,358.12*

Humour

If there's a chance it'll raise a chuckle, there's a good chance it'll catch your readers' attention. However, your subject lines still need to be in keeping with your business' voice, so bear that in mind and test your humorous subject line with a few people before you send it if you'd like an idea of what response it will lead to.

Example: *Why I'm banned from Madame Tussauds *angry face**

Being topical
News articles can provide great inspiration for any form of content marketing, and subject lines are no different. If the content of your email references something widely known that relates to your readers, consider using that as the attention-grabber in your subject line.

Speed is important here. The quicker you act after the news breaks, the more impactful it can be.

Example: *Something the Chancellor didn't tell you in the budget speech...*

Emojis and symbols
A report by Experian stated that 56% of brands using emoji in their email subject lines had a higher unique open rate (http://www.experian.com/blogs/marketing-forward/2012/07/17/thinking-about-using-symbols-in-your-email-subject-lines/).

Example: *Time is running out*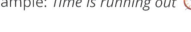

"IF THERE'S A CHANCE IT'LL RAISE A CHUCKLE, THERE'S A GOOD CHANCE IT'LL CATCH YOUR READERS' ATTENTION."

Re: and Fwd:

OK, this little 'tactic' has been around for a long time, so it's one to be used sparingly, but I'm including it here because it continues to work. Adding "Re:" or "Fwd:" (minus the quote marks) before a subject line gives the impression that you're replying to something sent previously, or forwarding something on.

You could use "Re:" to talk about whatever you've followed it with, or you could use "Fwd:" to send an earlier campaign again!

Example: *Re: Meeting for lunch*
Example: *Fwd: Would this be useful?*

COMMON MISTAKES

Choosing a great subject line and writing great content will set you on your way to creating email campaigns that get great results. However, it's easy to undo all the hard work you've put in with a few simple oversights. Here are some of the most common mistakes people make and how you can avoid them:

Sending without testing

Every once in a while, I'll see a marketing email from someone that's quickly followed by another, 10-15 minutes afterwards. The second email has a subject line that reads something along the lines of 'Oops, correct link this time!' or 'Sorry I got your name wrong'.

Why? They made a mistake in their email because they didn't take the time to test it or send themselves a preview before sending it out to their list. A number of the most common email marketing mistakes can be avoided by sending yourself a test message to check that the links and merge tags work correctly, or by sending a test to a friend or colleague to take a look over before you hit the 'Send campaign' button.

Subject lines that have no relevance to the email's content
There's more to a great subject line than just the subject line itself. The content of your email, especially the first line, should bring some context to the subject line you've used so that the two make sense together.

The mistake that many people make is choosing a subject line that is likely to get a good open rate (because it's interesting and intriguing), but then the first paragraph of content, and the remainder of the content too, make no sense when paired with that subject line.

Think about the subject line you've chosen and ask yourself what question your readers are likely to have when they see it. Then make sure you answer that question in the body of your email.

Getting merge codes wrong
Used correctly, adding a merge tag to include a person's name in a subject line can give your open rates a boost. However, it's also easy to get it very wrong. If you make a typo in your merge tag, miss a symbol or use the wrong field name your attempt at personalisation will miss the target and look embarrassing. Avoid this by sending yourself a test message first.

Overlooking the 'From' name and address
In addition to the subject line, your recipients will also see a 'From' name when your email arrives in their inboxes. What they

see here will influence their decision on whether to open, skip or delete your email, so it's important to pay attention to it.

Chances are, they'll remember your name rather than your company name. Plus it's much more personal if the message appears to come from a living person rather than a faceless corporate identity. With that in mind, use your full name as the 'From' name. In my case, "Nathan Littleton".

After they've read your message, perhaps they'll want to reply and ask you a question, pass comment or even make an enquiry. That's why it baffles me that so many messages are sent from 'no reply' or generic email addresses that don't respond directly to a person (noreply@, info@, sales@, support@, to name just a few). Use an email address that you, or someone within your team, can monitor regularly. Ideally, it'll be a name-based email address (joe@companyname.co.uk or joe.bloggs@companyname.co.uk) that corresponds with the 'From' name you've used.

Not considering the message preview
In many email applications, across desktops and mobile devices, the subject line is accompanied by the first line of text from the message itself. Some applications display more of this text than others, but it's usually between 15-20 words.

www.nathanlittleton.co.uk

OPENED

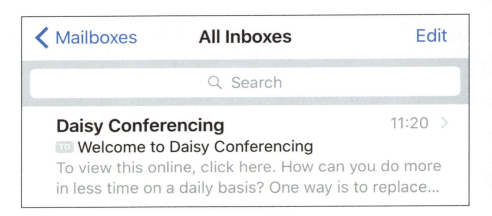

If it's in the app they're using, your recipients will read this text, so it'll be an additional factor in deciding whether to open your email or not.

You should make this text look indistinguishable from a one-to-one message, so the first element that's displayed should be a salutation such as 'Hi', 'Hey' or 'Dear' followed by the person's name (using a merge tag, explained above). The line following this shouldn't give too much away about what you want to say.

 IN MANY EMAIL APPLICATIONS, ACROSS DESKTOPS AND MOBILE DEVICES, THE SUBJECT LINE IS ACCOMPANIED BY THE FIRST LINE OF TEXT FROM THE MESSAGE ITSELF."

www.nathanlittleton.co.uk

To get this right, you need to remove anything from your content before the salutation that's text-based, such as 'View this message online' links and message summaries.

An often-overlooked element that may feature in the message preview is your header image, if you have one. It isn't strictly text-based, but most email marketing apps allow you to provide alternative text for images (to be shown if image display is turned off or they haven't been downloaded) and as such it is included in the message preview. While providing alternative text for images is generally a good practice, if it's an image that appears at the very top of your email, I'd suggest you avoid it.

Remember, you can send yourself a test message to see how it appears in your inbox, and if your app displays the first line of text next to the subject line, you'll be able to see for yourself what it looks like.

www.nathanlittleton.co.uk

BONUS: CALL TO ACTION TEXT

Once you've chosen a subject line that gets your email opened, and you've crafted an article or sales copy that's engaging and compelling, the final step in leading your readers to the web page you want them to visit is to have a strong call to action that tells them exactly what you want them to do next.

"Click here" just doesn't cut it. Neither does "Learn more". For the best results, you need something that catches the eye a little better and either explains the benefit they'll get from clicking on it or uses emotive language to draw them in.

As an added bonus to the 171 subject lines featured in this book, I've also compiled a comprehensive list of calls to action that you can swipe and deploy in your own campaigns.

FOR THE BEST RESULTS, YOU NEED SOMETHING THAT CATCHES THE EYE A LITTLE BETTER AND EITHER EXPLAINS THE BENEFIT THEY'LL GET FROM CLICKING ON IT OR USES EMOTIVE LANGUAGE TO DRAW THEM IN."

OPENED

Examples:

- Choose options
- Choose your size
- Choose colour
- Complete the 43-second form
- Contact us now
- Create a free account
- Download free eBook
- Download it now
- Free 30-day trial
- Get a free account
- Get an instant quote
- Get started now
- Get it now
- Get the facts
- Go!
- I want it
- Join today
- Listen here
- Save now
- See it in action
- Sign up for free
- Sign up now
- Start now
- Start the 37-second application
- Start your free trial today
- Start your 17-day trial for just £1

- Take a look
- Try it for free
- Try it now
- Try the free demo now
- View the deals
- View feature list
- View free report

ABOUT THE AUTHOR

Nathan is a marketer, professional speaker and author who specialises in helping businesses to grow by attracting and winning more customers.

Having started his first business at the age of just 12, he has become one of the UK's best and brightest young business figures, with more experience than most people twice his age. More than a decade on, he's worked with thousands of

 EACH YEAR NATHAN SENDS MORE THAN A MILLION EMAILS ON BEHALF OF HIS CLIENTS, AND HIS PROVEN TRACK RECORD HAS LED TO HIM WORKING WITH BUSINESSES RANGING FROM SMALL ACCOUNTANCY FIRMS TO INTERNATIONAL FRANCHISES."

www.nathanlittleton.co.uk

businesses across the UK and around the world to transform their online marketing and help them to generate better results.

Each year he sends more than a million emails on behalf of his clients, and his proven track record has led to him working with businesses ranging from small accountancy firms to international franchises. As an in-demand conference speaker, he also speaks regularly on different aspects of online marketing.

Web	www.nathanlittleton.co.uk
Email	hello@nathanlittleton.co.uk
LinkedIn	uk.linkedin.com/in/nathanlittleton/

NOTES:

OPENED

NOTES:

NOTES:

OPENED

NOTES: